ELECTRICITY

Investigating the Presence and Flow of Electric Charge

CHRIS WOODFORD Discarded

rosen publishing's
rosen central

New York

This edition first published in 2013 by:

The Rosen Publishing Group, Inc.
29 East 21st Street
New York, NY 10010

Copyright © 2013 by Brown Bear Books Ltd

Consultant: Don Franceschetti, Ph.D., Distinguished Service Professor, Departments of Physics and Chemistry, The University of Memphis, Memphis, Tennessee

Creative Director: Jeni Child
Picture Researcher: Helen Simm
Illustrators: Darren Awuah,
    Richard Burgess, and Mark Walker
Managing Editor: Tim Harris
Children's Publisher: Anne O'Daly
Production Director: Alastair Gourlay
Editorial Director: Lindsey Lowe

Library of Congress Cataloging-in-Publication Data

Woodford, Chris.
Electricity: investigating the presence and flow of electric charge/Chris Woodford.—1st ed.
    p. cm.—(Scientific pathways)
Includes bibliographical references and index.
ISBN 978-1-4488-7197-1 (library binding)
1. Electricity—Juvenile literature. 2. Electric charge and distribution—Juvenile literature. I. Title.
QC527.2.W684 2013
537—dc23

2011044495

Manufactured in the United States of America

CPSIA Compliance Information: Batch #S12YA: For further information, contact Rosen Publishing, New York, New York, at 1-800-237-9932.

PHOTOGRAPHIC CREDITS
Cover: Shutterstock

Corbis: Shelley Gavin 34; **DaimlerChrysler:** 37; **Getty Images:** Hulton Archive 21, 25; **Mary Evans Picture Library:** 6, 7, 10, 11t, 11b, 14, 15t, 16t, 18, 20, 23; **Photodisc:** 1, 4–5, 35; **Science & Society Picture Library:** 12, 24tl, 28b, 31; **University of Pennsylvania:** Smith Image Collection 8, 9bl, 9br, 13, 16b, 24tl, 26, 27, 28t, 30, 31b.

Illustrators: Darren Awuah, Richard Burgess, and Mark Walker

CONTENTS

<u>INTRODUCTION</u>

The quest to understand how electricity works has led to some of the most important discoveries and inventions of all time. At first, though, the mysteries of electricity baffled even the most brilliant thinkers.

PEOPLE OFTEN THINK OF electricity as a modern discovery: It is electricity that powers computers, cellular phones, and satellites in space. Yet scientists have known about simple kinds of electricity, such as static electricity, for more than two thousand years. Only in the last two or three hundred years, however, have people understood electricity well enough to put it to use.

During this time, scientists discovered that static electricity, produced when certain substances are rubbed against each other, and current electricity, which flows through wires, are really the same thing. They have also found that magnetism and electricity are related to each other and are part of a much larger phenomenon called electromagnetism. Scientists have figured out how to harness the power

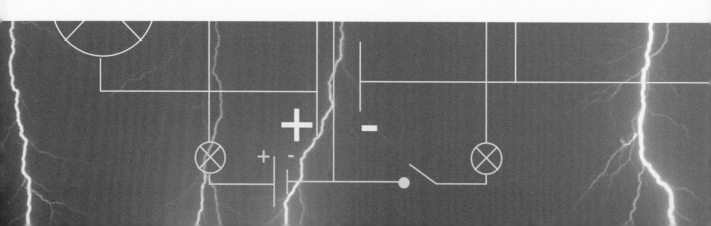

of electricity on a very large scale in big power plants. They have also mastered electricity on a very tiny scale by devising ways to control electrons inside computer circuits. Electrons are microscopic particles that move when electric currents flow.

How people came to understand electricity is a story of both science (understanding how the world works) and technology (using science to solve everyday problems). The great scientists who solved the mysteries of electricity were often also great inventors who were motivated by the idea of making life easier for people. Sometimes scientists came up with

important inventions. Sometimes inventors pushed the frontiers of science forward.

No single person discovered electricity. Instead, our modern ideas have been gradually put together over a long period as scientists built on the work of their predecessors. In some ways, science works like a never-ending relay race, as one generation of scientists passes on the baton of knowledge and discovery to the next. Although scientists know much more about electricity today than ever before, there are still many questions that must be answered before electricity can be understood fully.

1 STATIC AND FLOWING ELECTRICITY

Early scientists thought that electricity was a fluid (like water) that flowed from place to place, but they were not sure whether there was one kind of electric fluid or two.

THE STORY OF ELECTRICITY began around 600 BCE with ancient Greek thinker Thales of Miletus (625–546 BCE). Thales found that if he rubbed a piece of amber, it would pick up feathers and bits of cork as a magnet would with metal. Around 77 CE, Roman author Pliny the Elder wrote

SCIENCE AND STORIES

Pliny the Elder (23–79 CE; above) collected ideas about the world in his book *Natural History*, which was one of the first science encyclopedias. It contained not only science as people study it today, but also stories, superstitions, and ideas about magic.

STATIC ELECTRICITY

Static electricity is caused when electricity builds up in one place. If you walk across a nylon carpet, static electricity builds up on your body. If you then touch something metal, such as a faucet, you might feel a sudden electric shock in your finger. That shock is like a very tiny bolt of lightning that carries the static electricity from your body to Earth.

When rubber balloons are rubbed on a woolen sweater, static electricity builds up on their surface. This pushes the balloons apart.

ELECTRIC CHARGE

The amount of electricity something has is called its charge. If you rub a dry plastic rod two or three times, it gains a charge and it can pick up tiny bits of paper. If you rub it ten or twenty times, it gains much more charge and can pick up lots more (or bigger) pieces of paper.

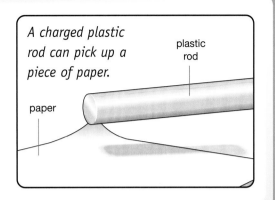

A charged plastic rod can pick up a piece of paper.

plastic rod

paper

about similar simple experiments with electricity in his book *Natural History*. These ancient thinkers had discovered static electricity.

It was not until the seventeenth century that people tried to understand what caused electricity. English doctor and scientist William Gilbert (1544–1603) carried out many experiments on both electricity and magnetism and was the first person to use the word "electricity." Another Englishman, Stephen Gray (1666–1736), found that some materials, such as amber, could hold an electric charge for a long time. Other materials, such as metals, could not store charge at all. This was how Gray discovered the difference between insulators and conductors.

INSULATORS AND CONDUCTORS

Insulators are materials like plastic and glass. They hold electricity, which flows through them very poorly or not at all. Conductors are materials, like metal, that do not hold electricity, but carry (conduct) it very well. Electric cables are made from a central wire, which carries the electricity, wrapped in a plastic insulator to keep people from getting electric shocks.

TWO ELECTRICITIES?

Hang a plastic ruler from a cotton thread and rub it a few times with a dry cloth. Now rub another ruler and bring it up to the first one. The two rulers push away from (or repel) one another. If you rub a glass rod and bring it up to the dangling ruler, however, the two pull toward (or attract) one another. An experiment like this one made Charles du Fay think there were two different kinds of electricity, one gained by materials like plastic and another gained by materials like glass.

WATSON'S WIRE

William Watson (1715–1787; left) carried out many experiments on electricity. In one of the most important of these, he showed that electricity could flow down a wire 2 miles (about 3 km) long. The wire stretched through the streets of London, England, and even crossed a bridge over the Thames River.

French chemist Charles François du Fay (1698–1739) thought electricity was caused by two kinds of electric fluids. He believed things gained an electric charge when they had more of one kind of electric fluid and less of the other kind. Not everyone believed this idea, however. In 1746, a British scientist named William Watson suggested that there was only one kind of electric fluid.

Du Fay and Watson had put forward two different theories (ideas suggested by scientists), but which one was correct? Was there one kind of electric fluid or two? Benjamin Franklin helped settle the issue. During the 1740s, he became fascinated by electricity and even gave up his work so that he would have time to study it. Like Watson, Franklin thought there was just one kind of electric fluid and invented the terms "positive" and "negative" to explain it. Objects that have a lot of electric fluid become negatively charged, while objects that have a little become positively charged. Franklin also proved that

lightning is a form of electricity with his famous kite experiment. This led him to invent the lightning rod, a long piece of metal that runs down the side of tall buildings to protect them from lightning strikes.

BENJAMIN FRANKLIN

Benjamin Franklin (1706–1790; below) was a distinguished statesman who helped draft the constitution of the United States. He was also an author, publisher, philosopher, and scientist. Apart from the lightning rod, he invented the rocking chair, the wood-burning Franklin stove, and bifocal eyeglasses. In 1770, he discovered the warm Atlantic Ocean current called the Gulf Stream.

FLYING HIGH

Franklin tried to prove that lightning was a huge electric spark by carrying out a very risky experiment—flying a kite in a thunderstorm. Although the kite and string became charged, no lightning struck the kite. If it had done so, Franklin probably would have been killed!

2 MAKING ELECTRIC CHARGE FLOW

The science of electricity took a dramatic new turn when two Italian scientists discovered that electric charge could be made to flow from one place to another.

BENJAMIN FRANKLIN HAD AN enormous influence on the study of static electricity. This was not only through his own work. During a visit to London, he met English scientist Joseph Priestley (1733–1804) and encouraged him to study electricity. Priestley's work, in turn, spurred on

HENRY CAVENDISH

A millionaire, English scientist Henry Cavendish (1731–1810; left) was nevertheless a shy and shabby figure, eccentrically dressed in a faded violet suit and old-fashioned hat. He loathed women, rarely spoke more than a few words, and seldom appeared in public. Yet his brilliant mind was constantly busy pondering important scientific ideas.

ELECTRIC FIELDS

A magnet creates a powerful but invisible force around it that can attract nearby objects made from certain metals. This is called a magnetic field. In much the same way, an electric charge creates an invisible electric field around itself.

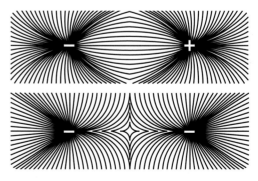

Lines of force spread out from positive (+) and negative (−) electric charges much like the lines of force produced by a magnet. Opposite charges attract and like charges repel each other.

other scientists, notably a Frenchman called Charles Augustin de Coulomb (1736–1806) and the Englishman Henry Cavendish. Coulomb and Cavendish helped discover how electric fields work.

Many of the early studies of electricity were made in England, but an Italian physician by the name of Luigi Galvani made the next major breakthrough. After he studied how electricity could make the muscles of animals jerk, he carried out a series of now-famous experiments with the legs of dead frogs. Galvani's findings led him to believe (incorrectly) that animals contained "animal electric fluid." He thought this fluid came from the brain and that the flow of fluid caused the muscles to move.

END OF THE GREAT GALVANI

Luigi Galvani (1737–1798) became a professor at the University of Bologna, Italy, at the age of only 25. A gentle and modest man, he quickly became a distinguished physician and scientist. In 1797 he refused to support Napoléon, the new head of state, and he lost his job, his salary, and his home. He died soon afterward at the age of 61.

GALVANI'S EXPERIMENTS

In one of his first electrical experiments, Galvani made a frog's legs twitch by touching them with a pair of scissors during a thunderstorm. He is better known, though, for another experiment (right), when he pushed brass hooks through a frog's legs, hung the legs on an iron railing, and the legs twitched. Galvani thought that "animal electricity" was responsible for this.

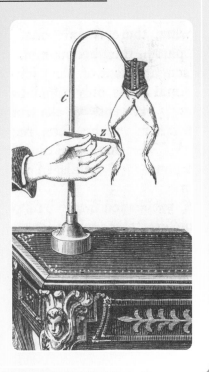

METALS AND BATTERIES

When two different metals are connected using a substance called an electrolyte, electricity is produced. This is the basic idea behind batteries, which were invented by Alessandro Volta. The first battery, known as a voltaic pile, was a "sandwich" made of alternate disks of silver, disks of cardboard soaked in saltwater (the electrolyte), and disks of zinc.

A copy of the original voltaic pile.

ELECTRIC CIRCUITS

When an electric charge builds up in one place, it is called static electricity. When something that has a static charge is connected with a conductor to something that has no charge, the charge flows from the statically charged object to the object with no charge. A flowing charge is known as an electric current or current electricity. Current electricity can also be made to flow continuously around a circular path known as an electric circuit.

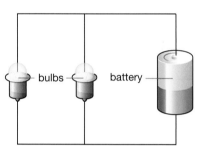

An electric circuit with two bulbs and one battery. The battery produces an electric current that causes the bulbs to light up.

Not everyone believed in animal electric fluid. Another Italian professor, Alessandro Volta (1745–1827), disagreed with Galvani's ideas. After he did experiments with different animals and different metals, he discovered that electricity could be made without animal tissue. Volta believed that an electric charge was produced when two different metals touched one another and made an electric circuit. Volta called this idea "metallic electricity," but he did not fully settle the question about animal electricity. As a result, some scientists continued to believe Galvani's ideas, and the argument over animal electricity and metallic electricity continued for many years.

Volta's research marked the beginning of a new scientific field called electrochemistry. This is the study of how electricity and chemistry work together. Its most important champion was the English chemist Humphry Davy. Davy built batteries that were similar to Volta's, only much bigger, to generate powerful electric currents (flows of electricity). Using a method called electrolysis, he passed these currents through chemical compounds and discovered a number of chemical elements, including sodium, potassium, and calcium. Through Davy, Volta's work led to great advances in chemistry.

HUMPHRY DAVY

The son of a woodcarver, Humphry Davy (1778–1829; right) is best remembered today for the Davy safety lamp—a device that miners could use without igniting dangerous gases underground. Yet his most important contribution to science was the discovery that electrolysis could split chemical compounds into their component elements.

ELECTROLYSIS

In a battery, electricity is produced by two different metals (electrodes) and a chemical (electrolyte) in between them. Electrolysis works in the opposite way. When two electrodes are dipped into a liquid compound (a combination of two or more elements) and a supply of electricity is connected across them, a chemical reaction takes place. This splits the compound into its separate parts. For example, electrolysis can be used to split water into the gases hydrogen and oxygen.

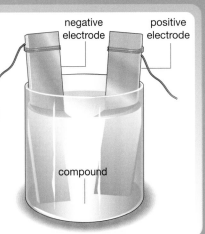

negative electrode

positive electrode

compound

3 THE DISCOVERY OF ELECTROMAGNETISM

Electricity and magnetism were once thought to be very different things. During the nineteenth century, scientists discovered that these two phenomena had much more in common than had once been supposed.

THROUGHOUT HISTORY, scientists noted similarities between electricity and magnetism. The ancient Greek philosopher Thales of Miletus (see page 6) studied both phenomena, as did English scientist William Gilbert. Scientists continued to treat electricity and magnetism as though they were

THALES AND MAGNETS

Thales (below) believed magnets had souls because, like people, they were powerful enough to move iron.

THE GALILEO OF MAGNETISM

William Gilbert (1544–1603) was given the nickname "the Galileo of magnetism" after he published a book that explained how magnets work. Gilbert was the first to suggest that Earth behaves like a giant magnet. He thought this explained why compass needles always point north. He was right.

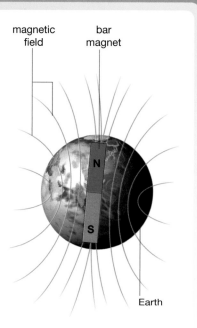

Like a bar magnet, Earth has a magnetic field with north (N) and south (S) poles.

separate things until the start of the nineteenth century.

One of the first people to suggest that there might be a link between electricity and magnetism was Italian philosopher and lawyer Gian Domenico Romagnosi (1761–1835). Around 1802, Romagnosi experimented with a Voltaic pile (see page 12) and a magnetic needle. The results of his experiments did not attract much attention because they were published in a little-known newspaper. The definite link between electricity and magnetism was made by Danish physicist Hans Christian Ørsted (1777–1851) almost twenty years later. Ørsted became famous for his discovery; Romagnosi is now largely forgotten.

ØRSTED'S EXPERIMENT

Ørsted first predicted the magnetic effect of an electric current in 1813, but it was not until the winter of 1819–1820 that he proved his theory. In a very simple experiment, he ran a metal wire underneath a compass needle. When he connected the wire to a battery and turned on the current, the compass needle flicked slightly before returning to its original position. The same thing happened when Ørsted switched off the current. He concluded that the electric current produced a magnetic field, and it was this field that made the compass needle move.

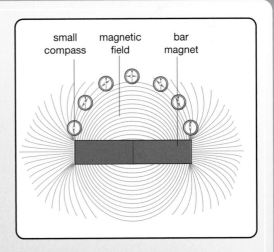

small compass   magnetic field   bar magnet

A compass needle will move as shown above when rotated around a bar magnet. Ørsted proved that an electric current has the same effect.

MATHEMATICAL GENIUS

Although largely self-taught, André-Marie Ampère (1775–1836; right) was a gifted child who, by the age of 12, had mastered all the mathematical knowledge then known. He became a math teacher at the age of 21, professor of physics and chemistry at 26, and professor of mathematics eight years later.

By September 1820, news of Ørsted's discovery had traveled to Paris, France. Math professor André-Marie Ampère immediately seized upon it. Over the next seven years, Ampère developed a detailed mathematical theory of electricity and magnetism. During his research, he discovered that if two wires carrying electric currents are placed close together, they will attract or repel one another because of the magnetism they produce. Ampère also invented the ammeter for measuring electric current.

An ammeter is a bit like a compass that can measure the size of an electric current. Inside an ammeter, a current passes through a coil of wire. The wire rotates between the poles of a magnet.

FARADAY, DAVY'S GREATEST DISCOVERY

Michael Faraday (1791–1867; right) started life as a poor blacksmith's son who sometimes had to survive a whole week on a single loaf of bread. At the age of 14, he found work as an assistant to a bookbinder. When he got the chance to attend the lectures of Sir Humphry Davy, Faraday took notes, bound them, and sent a copy to Davy. Some time later, Davy gave Faraday a job as his laboratory assistant, taught him chemistry, and helped him become one of the greatest scientists of the nineteenth century.

GENERATOR AND MOTOR

If an electric conductor is moved through a magnetic field, electric current will flow in the conductor. In an electric generator, a conductor such as a coil of wires is moved through a magnetic field made by magnets. This causes current to flow in the wires. In an electric motor, the electric current from a battery or other power source makes a coil of metal into an electromagnet. When placed between two magnets, the coil will turn because of the repelling force of opposing magnetic poles. A device called a commutator reverses the current every half turn to keep up the rotation. The continuous turning motion of the coil drives the motor.

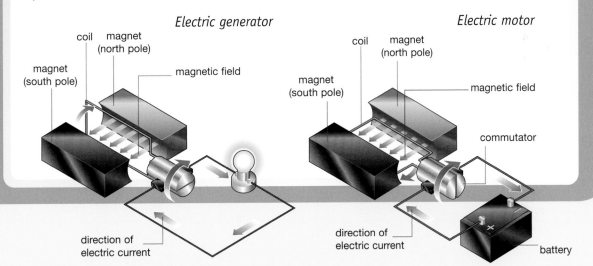

Electric generator

magnet (south pole)

coil magnet (north pole)

magnetic field

direction of electric current

Electric motor

magnet (south pole)

coil magnet (north pole)

magnetic field

commutator

direction of electric current

battery

This makes the needle rotate according to the strength of the current. The size of a current is measured in scientific units called amps (short for amperes), named for Ampère.

Ørsted had proved that electricity could make magnetism. About ten years later, self-taught British scientist Michael Faraday showed the opposite effect: magnetism could be used to make electricity. Faraday also showed how electricity and magnetism could work together to produce a pushing force. With these two discoveries, Faraday developed the basic science that later led to two important inventions: the electric generator and motor.

A BRILLIANT MIND

When James Clerk Maxwell (1831–1879; left) was a young boy, his tutor claimed he was dull and slow at learning. Nothing could have been farther from the truth. Maxwell had a brilliant mind and a superb memory. He published his first scientific paper at the age of only 14 and entered college at age 16. His outstanding scientific career has been compared in importance with those of the great scientists Sir Isaac Newton and Albert Einstein. Maxwell devoted the last five years of his life to publishing the scientific notebooks of an earlier genius of electricity, Henry Cavendish (*see* page 10.)

Scottish physicist James Clerk Maxwell turned Faraday's results into a complete theory that linked electricity and magnetism. Maxwell's theory explained everything scientists had found out about both electricity and magnetism—from the way Thales could pick up feathers with his charged piece of amber to Faraday's demonstration of the electric generator and motor.

Maxwell's theory is called "electromagnetism" and is based on four mathematical equations. Electromagnetism explains that electricity and magnetism are really two different aspects of the same phenomenon, like the head and the tail of the same animal. Both electric charges and magnetic poles (the ends of a magnet) can create an electromagnetic field that stretches out all around them.

Maxwell secured a reputation as a great scientist with his theory of electromagnetism. Apart from this, he also made a number of other important contributions to physics.

Maxwell published important work on optics (the study of light) and the theory of how gases store heat energy. As a young scientist still in his 20s, he developed a theory that the rings around the planet Saturn were made of small, separate particles. This theory was proved to be correct more than one hundred years later by a Voyager space probe.

MAXWELL'S EQUATIONS

In 1873, Maxwell published his theory of electromagnetism. It was a brilliant piece of science in which he summed up the entire science of electricity and magnetism in just four equations. Using complex math, Maxwell's equations describe how an electric charge creates an electric field, while the poles of a magnet create a magnetic field. The equations also show that a changing electrical field can produce magnetism and a changing magnetic field can produce electricity.

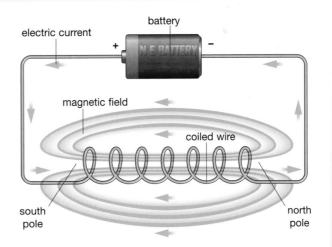

When an electric current flows through a coil of wire, it creates a magnetic field all around it. The field has a north pole and a south pole—just like a bar magnet. This electromagnetic phenomenon is explained completely by Maxwell's equations.

4 THE POWER OF ELECTRICITY

Until the nineteenth century, electricity was little more than a curiosity for scientists to study. When ingenious inventors discovered how to harness its power, the age of electricity truly began.

BEFORE THE 1800S, PEOPLE HAD no idea what electricity could be used to do. The crucial scientific breakthrough that brought about the age of electricity was made around the

JOULE'S OBSESSION

Unlike many scientists, James Prescott Joule (above) did not work at a university. As a wealthy man with a large private income, he funded his own research. Joule was so obsessed by energy that he even carried out energy experiments during his honeymoon. He kept his own steam engine at home for his research but had to get rid of it when the neighbors complained!

RESISTANCE

Conductors such as metals allow current to flow through them easily. They resist the flow of electricity very little, so they are said to have low electrical resistance. It is harder to make a current flow through insulators such as wood or plastic. These are said to have a high resistance. The theory of resistance was originally developed in the 1820s by German physicist Georg Simon Ohm (1787–1854).

The voltage produced by the battery in both cases is the same, but a more powerful resistor allows less current to flow through the circuit.

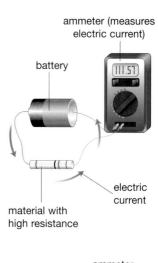

ammeter (measures electric current)

battery

electric current

material with high resistance

ammeter

battery

material with low resistance

middle of the nineteenth century by Scottish physicist James Prescott Joule (1818–1889). Joule proved that electricity is a type of energy, just like heat or light. In the 1830s, he carried out an experiment with electricity and heat. When he published his results in 1840, he showed how the resistance of an electric circuit could be used to turn a certain amount of electrical energy into the same amount of heat energy.

In the years that followed, Joule performed more work with energy. He became famous when he proved that one form of energy can be converted into exactly the same amount of a different type of energy. This important finding became known as the conservation of energy.

CONSERVATION OF ENERGY

The theory of energy conservation explains that energy cannot be created out of thin air or made to disappear completely—it can only be turned into other forms of energy. In other words, energy is always conserved (maintained). For example, when a moving automobile screeches to a halt, most of the kinetic (movement) energy that it had is converted into heat energy—the brakes heat up when the automobile slows down. In this illustration, power from a battery (**1**) is used to heat water into steam (**2**). The steam provides kinetic energy that turns a turbine (**3**). That kinetic energy is changed into electrical energy by a generator. Electrical energy can be used to power devices such as lightbulbs (**4**), sound systems (**5**), and electric heaters (**6**).

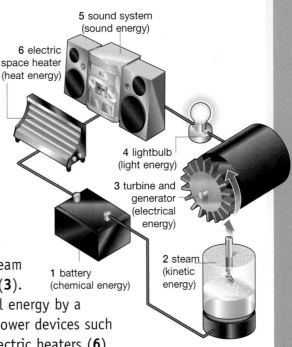

5 sound system
(sound energy)

6 electric space heater
(heat energy)

4 lightbulb
(light energy)

3 turbine and generator
(electrical energy)

2 steam
(kinetic energy)

1 battery
(chemical energy)

Electric motors provide an example of a way in which electricity can be turned into a useful form of power, because motors convert electrical energy into mechanical energy that can drive machines. Although the basic science behind motors was demonstrated by Michael Faraday, practical motors really developed through the work of British inventor William Sturgeon. Sturgeon developed the first practical electromagnet in 1825 by wrapping a length of wire many times around a piece of iron shaped like a horseshoe. When he passed an electric current through this device, Sturgeon found it could pick up pieces of metal up to twenty times its own weight. He also used an electromagnet as the main

WILLIAM STURGEON

Born to a life of grinding poverty, William Sturgeon (1783–1850) ran away to join the army. As a cadet, he taught himself science and made kites that could give people electric shocks. His claim to fame was the invention of the commutator, a device that allows an electric motor to rotate continuously in the same direction by reversing the electric current twice each time the motor turns around (*see* page 17.)

BUILD AN ELECTROMAGNET

An electromagnet is a magnet made by electricity. It is very easy to build your own. Take one 1.5-volt battery, about 12 inches (30 cm) of plastic-covered wire, and a thick metal nail. Wrap the cable tightly around the nail to make a coil. Connect the ends of the cable to the battery using clips or sticky tape. Try to pick up paper clips or other small pieces of metal with your magnet.

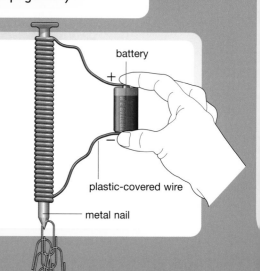

battery

plastic-covered wire

metal nail

THE ELECTRIC WEATHER FORECAST

America's great nineteenth-century physicist Joseph Henry (1797–1878) made many important contributions to science. In 1846, he became the first director of the Smithsonian Institution, where he began to make detailed observations of the weather. One of the first uses of Henry's electric telegraph was to transmit weather forecasts. This work eventually led to the formation of the U.S. Weather Bureau (now known as the National Weather Service).

component of his electric motor, which he invented in 1832.

Sturgeon was not the only scientist interested in motors. Joseph Henry greatly advanced their development by showing how it is possible to make much more powerful electromagnets (and thus electric motors) using large coils of fine wire. In the 1830s, he made a massive electromagnet for Yale University that could lift 2,086 pounds (946 kg); Sturgeon's electromagnet had been able to lift only 9 pounds (4 kg). Henry also demonstrated how electromagnets could be used to send information by building the first practical electrical telegraph.

DISABILITY AND DETERMINATION

Edison's deafness was one of the reasons he worked so hard. Apart from giving him a reason to prove himself, it spurred on a number of his inventions, including the improvements he made to the electrical telegraph. Edison (below) was someone for whom disability was no barrier to great achievement.

THE FIGHT OVER LIGHT

English chemist and engineer Joseph Wilson Swan (1828–1914) claimed to have invented the lightbulb in the 1870s, at about the same time as Thomas Edison. At first, Edison and Swan argued over who had invented the lamp. Later, they joined forces and set up a company together to profit from the invention.

Swan's lightbulb (left) and Edison's lightbulb (right).

One man is remembered more than any other for moving the world into the age of electricity: Thomas Alva Edison (1847–1931). While he was still very young, Edison started to have problems with his hearing. This meant he found it difficult to hear his teachers in school. Instead, he turned to books as his main source of learning.

One of Edison's first inventions was an improved version of the electrical telegraph. He went on to develop microphones, experimental electric railroads, movie cameras, and the invention for which he is best known —the electric lightbulb. Often described as a genius, he received nearly 1,100 patents (exclusive rights to one's inventions) in his lifetime.

Electric inventions would have been little use to people without a supply of electricity to power them. Here, too, Edison proved himself to be a pioneer. In 1882, he built a prototype power plant to generate electricity in London, England. Later the same year, Edison constructed the world's first permanent power plant on Pearl Street in New York City. Both of these plants produced electricity using coal-powered steam engines to drive large electric generators.

Although Edison played a key role in the development of electricity, he was much more of an inventor than a scientist. He was more concerned with making useful things than with finding out how those things actually worked.

GENIUS OR WORKAHOLIC?

When people said Edison was a genius, he replied: "Genius is one percent inspiration and ninety-nine percent perspiration." By this he meant that hard work and determination are often much more important to scientists and inventors than a brilliant mind. Edison liked work more than anything else—so much so that his family complained about how much time he spent in his laboratory.

5 HOW ELECTRICITY MOVES

Toward the end of the nineteenth century, scientists realized that electricity and magnetism could travel through space in the form of waves. This led rapidly to the development of radio and television.

THE ANCIENT GREEKS SAW electricity as static: something that stayed in one place. Galvani, Volta, and those who followed them showed that electricity could also flow down wires in the form of an electric current (see pages 10–13). Michael Faraday went even further and suggested electricity and magnetism could travel through space in waves.

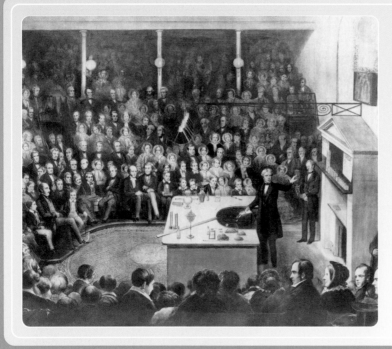

FARADAY'S VIBRATIONS

From the seventeenth century onward, scientists saw electricity as an invisible fluid that flowed from one place to another like water. In a public lecture in 1846, Faraday proposed that electricity actually moved through conductors in waves, or what he called "ray vibrations" (shaking movements).

ELECTROMAGNETIC RADIATION

Light, radio waves, and X-rays are all types of electromagnetic radiation that travel in waves at the speed of light. The different types of radiation are arranged on a spectrum (right) according to wavelength, starting with longest and lowest-energy wavelengths (radio waves) and moving up to the shortest and highest-energy wavelengths (gamma rays, such as from a nuclear explosion). Wavelength is the distance between the peaks or the troughs of a wave.

ELECTROMAGNETIC SPECTRUM

"mushroom" cloud

wave   peak
trough
wavelength

gamma rays
X rays
ultraviolet light
visible light
infrared rays (heat)
microwaves
radio waves

Building on Faraday's work, James Clerk Maxwell calculated the speed of these waves and found it was virtually the same as the speed of light. This made Maxwell think that light must be carried through the air by electromagnetism. He also theorized that there were other types of electromagnetic radiation that move at the speed of light.

In 1888, nine years after Maxwell's death, German physicist Heinrich Rudolf Hertz produced electromagnetic radio waves (the longest wavelengths of electromagnetic radiation) in his laboratory. With careful experiments, Hertz measured the length and frequency of the waves.

HERTZ AND FREQUENCY

Heinrich Hertz (1857–1894) gave his name to the hertz, a unit of frequency usually written Hz. The frequency of a wave is the number of complete waves that move past a given point in one second. An FM radio broadcast with a frequency of 100 MHz (one hundred million hertz) is carried by waves that arrive at the radio at a rate of one hundred million per second.

OLIVER LODGE

Oliver Lodge (1851–1940; left) is famous for inventing a device that could pick up radio signals traveling through air. He also believed people could pick up signals from the dead and devoted much of his time to researching the paranormal. After his son died in World War I (1914–1918), Lodge spent a lot of time trying to contact him through spiritual mediums.

He showed that radio waves could reflect (bounce off things) and refract (appear to bend through things) much like light, and that they traveled at the same speed as light.

Through his research, Heinrich Hertz discovered that electricity, or electromagnetic radiation, could be transmitted through the air without the need for wires. This proved to be a technological breakthrough as well as a scientific one, because it suggested that information might be carried from place to place in new ways.

In 1894, distinguished British physicist Oliver Lodge demonstrated a piece of electrical equipment called a coherer. This device made it possible to detect electromagnetic waves traveling in the air. An Italian named Guglielmo

HOW RADIO WORKS

Radio carries information invisibly through the air using electromagnetic waves. At a radio station, speech or music is turned into electrical signals by a microphone. These signals are then converted into radio waves. A powerful transmitter beams the waves out in all directions through a large antenna. Smaller antennas inside peoples' radios pick up the waves and turn them back into electrical signals. Finally, a loudspeaker turns the electrical signals back into speech or music.

An early radio wave detector called a Marconi coherer.

Marconi (1874–1937) took this invention much further. Marconi had become interested in radio waves at the age of 20 when he read an obituary of Heinrich Hertz. With homemade equipment, he soon managed to send radio signals over a distance of 1.5 miles (2.4 km). The Italian government was not interested in helping him develop the invention, so he moved to England. There, he went on to develop equipment that could send and receive information without wires over long distances. Marconi had invented the wireless, now better known as radio. When radio waves were used to carry pictures through the air as well as sound, television was born.

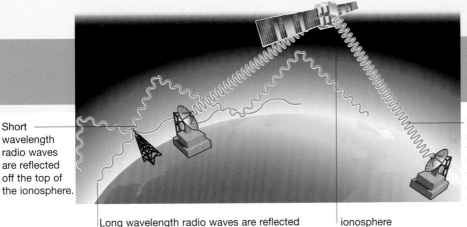

Short wavelength radio waves are reflected off the top of the ionosphere.

High-frequency signals pass through the ionosphere, so they are used for communications via satellites.

Long wavelength radio waves are reflected off the bottom of the ionosphere.

ionosphere

THE REACH OF RADIO

In 1901, Marconi succeeded in sending radio signals across the Atlantic from Cornwall, England, to St. John's, Newfoundland. Many people had refused to believe this was possible, because they thought Earth's curved surface would make the waves fly off into space. In fact, there is an electrically charged layer of Earth's atmosphere called the ionosphere, which acts like a huge curved mirror and reflects electromagnetic radio signals back to Earth. Earth in turn reflects the radio waves back to the ionosphere, and so on. In this way, radio waves can zigzag around the world, and the ionosphere makes it possible to pick up radio stations on the other side of Earth.

6 THE AGE OF ELECTRONICS

At the turn of the twentieth century, physicists discovered new particles called electrons, which seemed to carry electricity. This discovery led to the age of microelectronics and computers.

DESPITE EVERYTHING SCIENTISTS had learned about electricity by the end of the nineteenth century, they remained puzzled about electricity's causes. Was there one single thing behind electricity, or different things that caused static electricity, current electricity, and electromagnetism? In 1874, Irish physicist George Johnstone Stoney (1826–1911)

ELECTRON THEORY

The electron theory explains that both static electricity and current electricity are made by electrons. Static electricity is produced when electrons collect in one place. Electrons have a tiny negative charge, so a negatively charged object must have gained extra electrons. Similarly, a positively charged object must have lost electrons. Current electricity is caused when electrons move along a cable, carrying their tiny charges with them.

CLUMSY THOMSON?

Despite his brilliant mind, John Joseph Thomson (1856–1940; below) was very clumsy with his hands. His assistants encouraged him not to touch his experiments, and his wife did not let him do jobs around the house!

DISCOVERING THE ELECTRON

Thomson used a large glass bulb with a metal plate (or cathode) inside that was heated until it gave off rays. Thomson showed that these rays could be bent by electric or magnetic fields, which meant they must have an electric charge. He suggested that cathode rays were really microscopic particles. Thomson argued (correctly) that each particle (now known to be electrons) carried a small negative charge and must be present in every atom (*see* page 32.)

Thomson's original cathode ray tube.

suggested that there must be a tiny building block of electricity out of which bigger charges were made. Seven years later, German physicist Hermann von Helmholtz (1821–1894) argued that there were particles of electricity. Stoney went on to propose that electric current was really the movement of these small particles, each of which had a tiny charge. Stoney named these

particles "electrons" in 1891. The following year, Dutch physicist Hendrik Antoon Lorentz (1853–1928) helped turn these ideas into the electron theory of electricity.

All that remained was to prove electrons really existed. In 1897, British physicist J. J. Thomson discovered the electron when he was experimenting with cathode rays.

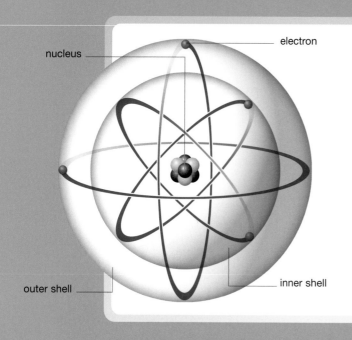

nucleus

electron

outer shell

inner shell

INSIDE THE ATOM

Shortly after his discovery of the electron, Thomson suggested that atoms are like plum puddings, with negatively charged electrons (plums) randomly dotted around positively charged matter (the pudding). Scientists now know that atoms are really made up of a central core of positive matter (the nucleus) around which electrons revolve (left).

Thomson's important find helped scientists unravel the mystery of the atom. It also helped to reveal the connection between electricity and electrons. This laid the foundations for a whole new technology—electronics.

The modern electronic age really began in 1906 when U.S. inventor Lee De Forest (1873–1961) invented the triode vacuum tube. This device could either amplify (make larger) tiny electric currents or switch them on and off. This ability to boost weak electrical signals later led to much improved radio sets and televisions. De Forest later became known as "the father of radio."

Vacuum tubes were also used in early computers until the 1940s, when three U.S. physicists, John Bardeen, Walter Brattain (1902–1987), and William Shockley (1910–1989), invented the transistor. This was a much better amplifier and switch than the

ELECTRIC OR ELECTRONIC?

Electrical appliances are simple things powered by electricity, such as lamps and stoves. Electronic appliances are usually more complex devices, such as radios, TVs, and computers. In an electrical appliance, electricity provides nothing more than power; in electronic equipment, electricity also controls how the appliance works. The most sophisticated types of electronic equipment, such as computers, use electrons to store and process numbers (digits). This is termed digital electronics.

vacuum tube: It was smaller, used less power, and was more reliable. In the 1950s, U.S. physicists Jack St. Clair Kilby (1923–2005) and Robert Noyce (1927–1990) figured out how to squeeze hundreds and later thousands of transistors onto a tiny chip of silicon called an integrated circuit. The next step was the single-chip computer, invented in 1969 by the American electrical engineer and inventor Ted Hoff (born 1937). It was this invention—the microchip—that led to the modern age of palm computers, digital watches, cellular phones, and compact electronic devices.

JOHN BARDEEN

Brilliant U.S. physicist John Bardeen (1908–1991) is so far the only person to have won the prestigious Nobel prize twice for the same subject. He shared the 1956 prize for physics with Brattain and Shockley. In 1972, he won the physics prize again with Leon Cooper and J. Robert Schrieffer for the theory of superconductivity. That theory explains how some materials can conduct electricity without resistance at very low temperatures.

7 FUTURE PROSPECTS

Scientists still have much to learn about electricity and magnetism. Technologists and inventors, meanwhile, are constantly discovering new ways of putting the science of electromagnetism to use.

ALTHOUGH THE DISCOVERY OF the electron was important, there is much still to be discovered about the nature of electricity and the way electrons behave.

In one major area of research, physicists have been trying to find out how the force that controls electromagnetism relates to the other three fundamental forces

FOUR FORCES

Four fundamental forces are believed to control the whole of nature: the electromagnetic force responsible for all electric and magnetic phenomena, the strong nuclear force that holds atoms together, the weak nuclear force that controls radioactivity, and the force of gravity that holds the planets in orbit around the Sun.

RICHARD P. FEYNMAN

One of the most colorful characters of modern physics, Richard P. Feynman (1918–1988) sometimes played conga drums during the lectures he gave. He shared the 1965 Nobel prize for physics for the QED theory. Just before he died, he played a major role in explaining the *Challenger* space shuttle explosion, which killed seven astronauts in 1986.

LIGHTNING AND GLOBAL WARMING

Physicists at the Massachusetts Institute of Technology (MIT) are studying global warming by measuring how many times lightning strikes around the world. Global warming is thought to increase the irregularity of the weather and make lightning more common, so this data could provide valuable evidence regarding how fast Earth is warming up.

CONDUCTING PLASTIC

Plastics are inexpensive to make, but they do not usually conduct electricity. Although plastics are useful for making electrical insulation, metals—which tend to be expensive—must be used to make electrical components. All that may soon be about to change. The 2000 Nobel prize for chemistry was won by a team of scientists who showed how a new type of plastic could be made to conduct electricity. The discovery could lead to much cheaper computer components.

of nature. One of the most important developments in this area was the theory of quantum electrodynamics (QED), put forward in the 1940s by U.S. physicist Richard P. Feynman. This theory explains how electrons behave when they move around inside electromagnetic fields.

The science of electricity often still offers up surprises. Two hundred years after Benjamin Franklin's kite experiment, physicists continue to discover new things about lightning, for example. Even the idea that insulators do not conduct electricity had to be revised in 2000 with the invention of a new type of plastic.

SUPERCONDUCTIVITY

In 1908, Danish physicist Heike Kamerlingh Onnes (1853–1926) found that some materials lose their electrical resistance if they are cooled down to very low temperatures approaching absolute zero (–459 °F or –273 °C, theoretically the lowest temperature that can ever be reached). This makes them much better carriers of electricity, or superconductors.

MAGLEV TRAINS

Unlike conventional trains, which rest on the track as they move and are slowed by friction, magnetic levitation (maglev) trains hover above the track, or rail, suspended by a magnetic field created by powerful electromagnets.

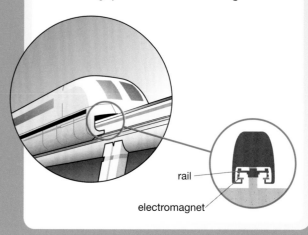

rail

electromagnet

Ever since the discovery of superconductivity in 1908, scientists have tried to develop materials that conduct electricity without resistance at higher temperatures. In 1986, high-temperature superconductors were invented that could bring the benefits of superconductivity at more easily reachable temperatures. These are likely to prove useful in faster computers and high-speed maglev trains that float along their tracks at up to 360 mph (580 kph).

Developments such as these aim to make electricity a more useful part of everyday life. Electricity may also prove useful in another way: protecting our fragile planet from environmental problems such as pollution and global warming (the way Earth is believed to be getting warmer when people use fossil fuels such as oil and coal). One solution to these problems may be to develop very efficient fuel cells that make clean electricity from hydrogen gas.

Although electricity has brought enormous benefits for humankind, there are some concerns that electromagnetic radiation could harm people's health. Many scientists are currently trying to find out whether electricity is really as safe as it seems.

With so much research still being conducted and so much still to discover, one thing is clear: The story of electricity has only just begun!

This bus is powered not by a conventional diesel engine but by a fuel cell.

FUEL CELLS

A fuel cell is a bit like a battery that never goes dead. It uses a continuous supply of fuel (usually hydrogen gas pumped in from a tank) to make electricity from a chemical reaction. Fuel cells have been used in spacecraft, but they are still too expensive for use in most automobiles and homes.

HEALTH SCARE?

Cellular phones, high-voltage power lines, and electrical appliances give off electromagnetic radiation. Some people believe that this could cause serious illness including leukemia. The World Health Organization studied this problem. In May 2011 it announced that there was limited evidence of cellphone users being at risk from electromagnetic radiation.

LEMON BATTERY

GOALS

1. Use a lemon to build a working battery.
2. Explore how electricity flows.
2. Test how well your lemon battery works in different conditions.

1 Take the lemon, and push on it gently while rolling it along a table top. This releases the juice inside. Take care not to break the skin of the lemon.

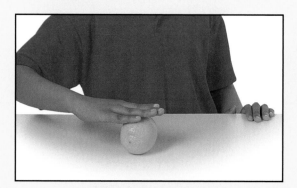

2 Using the wire clippers, cut a 2-inch (5cm) piece of copper wire. You might want to ask an adult to help you do this. Gently push the wire about 1 inch (2.5cm) into the lemon.

3 Straighten out the paper clip. Gently push the paper clip about 1 inch (2.5cm) into the lemon. Try to get the paper clip as close as you can to the copper electrode without touching it.

! **SAFETY TIP**
The lemon will not generate enough electricity to hurt—but take care when touching your tongue to the wires so that you don't cut yourself.

4 Roll your tongue around your mouth so it is nice and wet. Now, gently touch your tongue to both wire electrodes at the same time. You should feel a slight tingling sensation. Electricity produced by the lemon battery is flowing through your tongue!

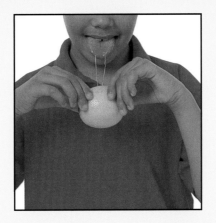

USING AN AMMETER

An ammeter measures current and displays it in amps, and a voltmeter measures voltage and displays it in volts. Ammeters and voltmeters come in two types. Some of them have pointers that swing back and forth across a dial. When a current passes through this type of ammeter, it generates magnetism, which makes the pointer move a bit like a compass needle. Other types of meters have digital displays (like the one we have used in this activity), and they measure current and voltage with electronic circuit boards instead of magnetism.

TROUBLESHOOTING

What if I can't feel a tingling sensation in my tongue?

First, make sure you are using a fresh, moist lemon. You may have to try a couple of different lemons before you get a nice juicy one. Place the wires very close together, and make sure your tongue is moist before touching it to the wires. Sometimes, using thicker copper wire will also make it easier to feel the current.

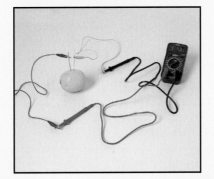

5 If you have an ammeter or voltmeter, use the electric wires with alligator clips to connect one terminal of the voltmeter to the paper clip and the other terminal to the copper electrode. If the meter shows a negative reading, you have connected your circuit the wrong way around. Swap the connections. Write down the reading in a notebook.

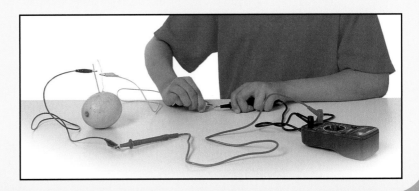

TIMELINE

	6000 BCE	300 CE
Atoms and Molecules	**2500 BCE** Tin ore is smelted in Turkey **4th century BCE** Greek philosopher Democritus believes the world is composed of tiny particles that cannot be divided	**1450** European metalworkers work out how to separate lead and silver ores
Electricity	**271 CE** The compass is first used in China; it works by detecting Earth's magnetic field	**1180** The first reference to the magnetic compass in Western writing is in Alexander Neckam's *Concerning Natural Things (De Naturis Rerum)*
Evolution		
Genetics		
Geology	**500 BCE** Xenophanes of Colphon (Greece) discovers that land can rise when he finds fossils of seashells on mountaintops	**1517** The Italian scientist Girolamo Fracastoro suggests that fossils are the remains of long-dead plants and animals
Gravity	**1450 BCE** Egyptians devise a water clock, based on the principle of dripping water **330 BCE** Aristotle believes that the Sun and planets orbit Earth	**1345** Dutch engineers use windmills to pump water out of areas that are being reclaimed from the sea
Light	**6000 BCE** People in Italy make mirrors from a rock called obsidian **1361 BCE** Chinese astronomers record a solar eclipse	**1021** Arab mathematician Alhazen writes about the refraction of light **1304** Theodoric of Freibourg, a German scientist, works out how rainbows form
Medicine	**2500 BCE** Chinese doctors begin using a pain-killing technique called acupuncture **1550 BCE** Egyptians are using about 700 drugs and medications	**365** Mechanical cranks are used to set broken bones in Greece **850** An Arab physician writes about eye disorders and treatments
Context	**c.3500 BCE** The wheel is invented in Mesopotamia **2630 BCE** Egyptians begin building the pyramids **776 BCE** The first Olympic Games are held in Greece **117 CE** Roman Empire reaches its greatest extent	**c.900** Mayan civilization in Mesoamerica collapses **1453** The Byzantine age comes to an end with the fall of Constantinople

1709 A model hot-air balloon is made in Brazil
1714 Gabriel Fahrenheit constructs a mercury thermometer

1738 Daniel Bernoulli proposes a kinetic theory of gases
c.1787 French physicist Jacques Charles draws up Charles's Law of gas volumes

1701 Edmond Halley draws up a map of Earth's magnetic field
1729 Stephen Gray explains electrical conductors and insulators

1742 Benjamin Franklin demonstrates the electrical nature of lightning
1800 Alessandro Volta develops the voltaic pile electric battery

1807 Humphry Davy uses electrolysis to isolate potassium and sodium
1822 André-Marie Ampere works out the laws of the movement of electricity

1809 Lamarck wrongly states that characteristics acquired during life are inherited by offspring
1831–36 Charles Darwin on HMS *Beagle*

1760s Robert Bakewell improves farmstock by selectively breeding animals

1831 Robert Brown is the first scientist to describe a cell nucleus

1691 Naturalist John Ray believes fossils are ancient life-forms

1793 Mammoth remains are found in Siberian permafrost

1811 Schoolgirl Mary Anning discovers the first fossil ichthyosaur
1815 Eruption of Mount Tambora in Indonesia modifies climates worldwide

1609 Johannes Kepler draws up laws of planetary motion
c.1665 Isaac Newton formulates his law of gravity

1665 Robert Hooke proposes that light travels in waves
1671 Isaac Newton shows that a prism splits light into a spectrum

1811 William Wollaston invents the *camera lucida*
1839 Louis Daguerre invents a kind of photograph taken on metal plates

1628 Physician William Harvey explains the circulation of blood
1721 Smallpox inoculation is carried out in North America

1745 The French surgeon Jacques Daviel successfully removes a cataract from a patient's eye—the first time this has happened

1805 Japanese physician Seishu Hoanoka performs surgery with general anesthesia
1811 Charles Bell pioneers study of the nervous system

1630 English Puritans colonize Massachusetts Bay
1665 Bubonic plague kills one-fifth of London's population

1787 The United States Constitution is adopted
1789 The French Revolution begins with the storming of the Bastille

1803 The Louisiana Purchase doubles the size of the United States
1833 A law is passed in Britain to abolish slavery in the British Empire

1600   **1730**   **1800**   **1850**

TIMELINE

Atoms and Molecules	**1892** James Dewar invents the vacuum bottle **1896** Henri Becquerel discovers radioactivity **1897** Physicist J.J. Thompson is the first person to identify electrons	**1905** Albert Einstein publishes his special theory of relativity **1910** The existence of the nucleus of an atom is proven by Ernest Rutherford
Electricity	**1877** American engineer Thomas Edison invents the phonograph **1885** American electrical engineer William Stanley makes the first transformer	**1923** John Logie Baird makes a type of television
Evolution	**1856** Male Neanderthal skeleton found; it differs in important ways from modern human skeletons **1859** Charles Darwin publishes *On the Origin of Species*, arguing his case for evolution	**1908** Marcellin Boule reconstructs a skeleton of a Neanderthal person **1926** Hermann Muller creates genetic mutations in fruit flies, using x-rays
Genetics	**1865** Gregor Mendel, an Austrian monk, puts forward his laws of inheritance; they are published the following year	**1909** Danish botanist Wilhelm Johannsen defines a gene **1913** Chromosome mapping is pioneered by Alfred Sturtevant
Geology	**1860** The first fossil *Archaeopteryx* is found **1883** Mount Krakatoa, in Indonesia, erupts; it is one of the largest volcanic eruptions in recorded history	**1913** Earth's age is calculated at 4.6 billion years by geologist Arthur Holmes **1935** Richter scale proposed to measure earthquake intensity
Gravity	**1851** Léon Foucault builds a pendulum (Foucault's pendulum) that shows Earth's rotation. **1891** John Poynting, an English physicist, works out the value of the gravitational constant	**1927** Georges Lemaitre suggests the universe originated with a "big bang"
Light	**1877** Joseph Swan, an English physicist, develops the first electric light bulb **1882** Albert Michelson calculates the speed of light to within 0.02 percent of the correct value	**1905** Albert Einstein publishes his special theory of relativity **1935** Transparency film invented by American amateur photographers
Medicine	**1885** Louis Pasteur manufactures a rabies vaccine **1898** The cause of malaria, the protozoa *Plasmodium*, is discovered by physician Ronald Ross **1903** X-rays first used to treat cancerous tumors	**1929** Hormone estrogen first isolated **1934** Radio waves used to treat cancer **1943** Kidney dialysis machine built by Willem Kolff
Context	**1861–1865** American Civil War **1876** The Sioux Army of Sitting Bull defeats U.S. forces at the Battle of Little Bighorn **1897** The Klondike Gold Rush begins	**1901** Guglielmo Marconi makes the first transatlantic radio broadcast **1914–1918** World War I **1939–1945** World War II

1850 **1900**

1952 The first hydrogen bomb is exploded on an atoll in the central Pacific
1960 First optical identification of a quasar
1967 Domestic microwave ovens are sold in U.S.

1961 The first silicon chips are manufactured
1962 The first national live TV broadcast, a speech by President Truman in San Francisco
1975 First commercial personal computers sold

1960 Remains of human ancestor *Homo habilis* discovered in Tanzania
1983 Fossils of a 16-million-year-old ancestor of humans are found by Meave Leakey in Africa

1953 The structure of DNA is discovered by Francis Crick and James Watson
1959 Down syndrome discovered to be caused by an extra chromosome

1977 Frozen body of a baby mammoth found in Siberian permafrost

1957 The first satellites, Sputnik 1 and Sputnik 2, are sent into orbit around Earth by the Soviet Union
1969 Astronauts Armstrong and Aldrin "bounce" on the Moon's surface, showing that gravity is less there

1955 Indian scientist Narinder Kapany invents optical fibers for carrying light long distances
1962 Light-emitting diode (LED) invented

1950 Link between smoking and lung cancer found
1958 Ultrasound scans are introduced to examine unborn babies
1967 The first successful heart transplant

1955–1975 Vietnam War
1968 Martin Luther King assassinated in Memphis
1969 Neil Armstrong and Buzz Aldrin are the first people to walk on the Moon's surface

1994 American scientists discover a subatomic particle that they call the top quark
2004 A "supersolid" is discovered by American scientists—it flows through another material without friction

1990 Work begins on developing the World Wide Web
2007 American scientists create flexible batteries by weaving microscopic tubes of carbon into paper

1993 The oldest-known human ancestor, *Ardipithecus ramidus*, is discovered by Berkeley scientists
2003 Footprints of an upright-walking human, who was alive 350,000 years ago, are found in Italy

1994 The first genetically modifed tomato is sold in the U.S.
1996 A sheep named Dolly is cloned in Edinburgh
1998 Human stem cells are grown in a laboratory
2000 Human genome is roughly mapped out

1996 Signs of microscopic life are found in a meteorite that originated from Mars
1997 Fossils of *Protarchaeopteryx*, a birdlike reptile, are found
2000 The fossil remains of a dinosaur's heart are found

1992 Scientists at the University of Pisa, Italy, make the most accurate calculation of the acceleration due to gravity

1998 Lasers are first used by American dentists for drilling teeth
2005 Flashes of light are discovered to create X-rays

1983 The human immunodeficiency virus (HIV) is discovered
1987 The first heart-lung-liver transplant is carried out by a team of British surgeons
2000 Works begins on making the first artificial heart

1989 Communist regimes across Europe collapse
1997 Diana, Princess of Wales, killed in a car accident in Paris
2001 Attack on the World Trade Center in New York
2008 Barack Obama elected first African–American president of U.S.

1950   **1990**   **2010**

KEY PEOPLE

André-Marie Ampère (1775–1836)

Ampère was a French physicist and mathematician who founded the science of electromagnetism. He was born in Lyons, the son of a wealthy merchant who was later executed in the French Revolution. Ampère began to experiment on what he called "electrodynamics" (electromagnetism) in 1820, having heard that an electric current passing through a wire could move the needle of a magnetic compass. Seven years later he announced what we now call Ampère's law, concerning the magnetic forces between wires carrying an electric current. The unit of current, the amp (A), is named for him.

Henry Cavendish (1731–1810)

Cavendish was born in France, to English parents, and went on to study at Cambridge University. He was shy and very modest about his scientific revelations, many of which were only discovered after his death. By combining metals with strong acids, Cavendish made hydrogen gas, which he studied. Although others had already isolated hydrogen, Cavendish recognized that it was an element, which he called "inflammable air." His electrical experiments led him to discover the concept of electric potential, the relationship between electric potential and current, now called Ohm's Law, and much more.

Humphry Davy (1778–1829)

Davy was born in Penzance, England, and had only a limited school education. He became an apprentice to a ship's surgeon, then taught himself chemistry, and—in 1797—discovered the anesthetic effect of nitrous oxide. He began to experiment with electrolysis, using the new electric battery invented by Alessandro Volta. Davy broke water into its component elements of hydrogen and oxygen, and later isolated the elements sodium, potassium, barium, boron, calcium, magnesium, and strontium. In 1815 he invented the miner's safety lamp (Davy lamp), which enabled miners to work safely in the presence of flammable gases.

Thomas Edison (1847–1931)

Edison was one of the greatest inventors of his age. By the time he died, he had more than 1,300 patents to his name. He was born in Milan, Ohio, and was taught at home by his mother. As a teenager, he became interested in the telegraph and was soon inventing his own equipment. Edison set up a laboratory at Menlo Park, New Jersey, where he made some of his best-known inventions, including the phonograph and the electric light bulb. He was the first person to realize the value of electric power and opened the world's first permanent electric power plant in New York in 1882.

Michael Faraday (1791–1867)

Faraday was an English physicist who had little formal education but went on to become one of the greatest scientists of his time. His many discoveries included the organic substance benzene, the laws of electrolysis, the dynamo, and the transformer. The dynamo and the transformer both made use of the relationship between magnetism and electricity, which was later to become so important in the development of microphones and loudspeakers. Faraday showed that moving a coil of wire in a magnetic field produces an electric current (as in a moving-coil microphone) and the opposite—passing a current through a coil in a magnetic field—causes the coil to move (as in a loudspeaker).

William Gilbert (1544–1603)

English-born Gilbert is considered to be one of the pioneers of the study of electricity. He studied static electricity, using amber, and called its effect the "electric force." Gilbert incorrectly believed that electricity and magnetism were two different forces. He was also an influential astronomer, explaining that the apparent motion of the stars is caused by Earth's rotation.

Heinrich Hertz (1857–1894)

Hertz was a German physicist who discovered a new type of radiation—radio waves—in 1887. He clarified Maxwell's electromagnetic theory of light and was the first to demonstrate the existence of electromagnetic waves. Hertz also showed that radio waves could be transmitted through different types of materials, and were reflected by others. This discovery would eventually lead to the invention of radar. The unit for frequency, the hertz (Hz) was named for him after his death at the age of 36.

Guglielmo Marconi (1874–1937)

Marconi, often called the "father of radio," was born and educated in Bologna, Italy. He began to experiment in the summer of 1894 when he built a storm alarm made up of a battery, a device called a coherer, and an electric bell; the bell sounded if there was lightning nearby. The following year he was able to transmit signals over a hill, a distance of about 1.5 miles (2.4 km). Transmission distances became longer as his equipment became more sophisticated. In 1901 he was able to transmit signals in Morse code across the Atlantic Ocean from Cornwall, England, to the United States.

James Clerk Maxwell (1831–1879)

Scottish physicist Maxwell was born in Edinburgh and attended the university in that city before moving first to Cambridge University then to Aberdeen University, where he was a professor at the very young age of 25. His most productive period was while he was at King's College, London, between 1860 and 1865. Then, he would often attend lectures at the Royal Institution, where he came into regular contact with Faraday. It was during this period that Maxwell predicted the existence of electromagnetic radiation.

Pliny the Elder (23–79)

Pliny the Elder was a Roman author, naturalist, and philosopher, as well as a naval and army commander in the early Roman Empire. The *Naturalis Historia*, published probably in 79, is one of the largest single works to have survived from the Roman empire to the modern day. It covers most of what the Romans knew about science.

J. J. Thomson (1856–1940)

Joseph John Thomson was born near Manchester, England. He trained as a railroad engineer, before attending Cambridge University. Thomson deflected cathode rays with electric and magnetic fields, and he showed that they travel more slowly than light waves. He also discovered that cathode rays consisted of minuscule negatively charged particles, which he called "corpuscles." Although another scientist (George Stoney, 1826–1911) had already predicted the existence of these particles and called them electrons, it was Thomson who provided the proof.

Alessandro Volta (1745–1827)

Count Alessandro Giuseppe Antonio Volta was born in Como, Italy. Unlike most of his male relatives, who became priests, Volta decided to study electricity. In 1774 he invented the electrophorus, a device for storing static electricity. But his best-known invention was the first electric battery, which consisted of a pile of alternating disks of copper and zinc, separated by pieces of cloth soaked in salt solution. It became known as a voltaic pile. Volta died in 1827, some years before the SI unit of potential difference—the volt (V)—was named to honor him.

GLOSSARY

ampere The standard unit for measuring electrical current.

amplify To increase the height of a wave, such as a radio wave.

atom The smallest part of an element that can exist. It is made up of protons and neutrons in a nucleus, surrounded by orbiting electrons.

battery A device that can store electricity using chemical energy.

charge The amount of electricity something contains.

circuit The path around which electric current flows.

compound A substance made of two or more elements.

conductor A material that allows electricity to flow through it very easily.

current electricity The movement of electrical charge through a circuit.

electric shock A sudden jolt or tingling sensation when electricity flows through a person's body.

electrolysis A method of splitting up substances into their component chemical elements using electricity.

electrolyte A liquid, such as that in a battery, which can conduct electricity and be separated by electrolysis.

electromagnet A temporary magnet produced using an electric current.

electromagnetic radiation A wave of electricity and magnetism that travels at the speed of light.

electromagnetism The combined theory of electricity and magnetism.

electron A tiny, negatively charged particle inside an atom that carries electricity.

electronics The study of electrons and how they work in electric circuits.

element A substance that cannot be split into two or more different parts by a chemical reaction.

energy The property of an object that gives it the ability to work against forces.

experiment A test of a scientific theory usually carried out in a laboratory.

field The spreading out of electromagnetic effects into the space surrounding electric charges and magnets.

filament A wire that heats up and gives off light when electricity flows through it.

force A pushing or pulling action that causes a change in an object's motion or shape.

generator A device that turns mechanical energy into electricity.

insulator A material that conducts electricity poorly or not at all.

ionosphere An electrically charged part of Earth's atmosphere that bounces or reflects radio waves around the planet.

molecule A group of two or more atoms that unite to form a chemical unit.

motor A device that converts electricity into mechanical energy.

negative charge An electric charge created when electrons are gained.

positive charge An electric charge created when electrons are lost.

resistance The way a material tries to stop an electric current flowing through it.

static electricity A build up of electric charge in one place.

superconductor A material that loses its electrical resistance when it is cooled to an extremely low temperature.

theory A scientific explanation of why something works.

transistor An electronic device that can switch currents on and off or amplify them.

FOR MORE INFORMATION

BOOKS

Bailey, Jacqui. *How Do We Use Electricity?* Mankato, MN: Smart Apple, 2007.

Bateman, Graham (ed.). *Introducing Physics: Electricity and Electronics.* Redding, CT: Brown Bear Books, 2010.

Cheshire, Gerard. *Electricity and Magnetism.* Mankato, MN: Smart Apple, 2007.

Dreier, David. *Electrical Circuits: Harnessing Electricity.* Minneapolis, MN: Compass Point, 2008.

Galiano, Dean. *Electric and Magnetic Phenomena.* New York, NY: Rosen, 2011.

Mahaney, Ian F. *Electricity.* New York, NY: Rosen 2007.

Reilly, Kathleen. *Energy: 25 Projects Investigate Why We Need Power and How We Get It.* Silver Spring, MD: Nomad, 2009.

Saunders, Nigel. *Exploring Electricity and Magnetism.* New York, NY: PowerKids Press, 2008.

Sobey, Ed. *Robot Experiments.* Springfield, NJ: Enslow, 2011.

Somervill, Barbara. *Electrical Circuits and Currents.* Chicago, IL: Heinemann Raintree, 2008.

WEB SITES

Due to the changing nature of Internet links, Rosen Publishing has developed an online list of Web sites related to the subject of this book. This site is updated regularly. Please use this link to access this list:

http://www.rosenlinks.com/scipa/elec

INDEX